Alderwick's sense of language is quie[...]
of what it means to be a broken hu[...]
surreality; a blue whale swims insi[...]
moonlight. And even the bounds of [...]
'learned to read the stars,' for 'those s[...]
shit...' And yet there's a certain kind [...]
a longing, at times wistful, at others [...]
tangible and real. Let these poems speak to how we all want to find moments of
being with rather than alone — how 'this would be a perfect place / for a photo,
a memory,' of that for which we earnestly desire.

— Ina Cariño, author of *Feast*

Comic without being flippant, intimate without being sweet, these are poems
of remorse and tenderness which come alive on the page. Alderwick's attention
to the quiet moments of deferral or joy that characterise our relationships are
wonderfully evocative, and he is adept at the kind of surreal fable which makes
a reader consider their own capacity for magic.

— Jack Warren, author of *Rude Mechanical*

Simon Alderwick's poetry is like playing your favorite video game all night long
without a care in the world. Like binge watching '80s horror movies with your
crush under the stars. It's going home after a long day of work and blasting
Metallica through your stereo. It's packing a cooler full of ice cold beer to go
to the beach with your buds. Which is to say, *ways to say we're not alone* is a
chokeslam straight to the heart and it's beautiful.

— Shawn Berman, author of *At the Movies*

Simon Alderwick's poems fizz with a deep uncertainty and moments of imagistic
magic. These are poems of faith and love, reminding us that, 'not all prayers are
answered' and bodies 'look perfect covered in droplets' of water. A blue whale
is found in a crisp packet — Alderwick's poems crackle with a sense of the
mythical and invite readers to be children again, living in wonder. These are
narratives. Poems that have a cinematic intensity. Stories where the fragility of
our lives stains each noun and verb. One aspect of Alderwick's work that I'll be
stealing is his use of repetition. The way it lends his poems a fierce and brooding
music. A music that will call you back to re-read and re-read. A haunting debut.

— Marvin Thompson, author of *Road Trip*

ways to say we're not alone is a powerfully immersive collection bringing together
themes of modernity, humanity, home, storms, climate and nature. Its dark and
intimate tone pulls us into these poems, with an evocative dreamlike quality
unleashing memories, longing, despair, nostalgia weighted with hope, beauty
and salvation. Alderwick's voice is distinctively fresh and honest, with a searing
touch of vulnerability he manages to bind visceral emotions, tenderness and
humour masterfully to draw us in, surprise, and provide solace and connection.
Exploring love, relationships, family, estrangement, sacrifice; his openness
allows us to relate to poetics, the kindness of strangers, moments of desolation
and deep torment; how we keep going, how to be ourselves.

— Louise Mather, author of *The Dredging of Rituals*

ways to say we're not alone

simon alderwick grew up in Kingston, Surrey. He now lives in Oxford with his wife and daughters, having spent the last ten years living between England, the Philippines and Wales. *ways to say we're not alone* is his first pamphlet.

ways to say we're not alone

simon alderwick

Broken Sleep Books

ISBN: 978-1-916938-06-9

Cover designed by Stuart McPherson

Edited by Aaron Kent

Typeset by Aaron Kent

Broken Sleep Books Ltd
Rhydwen
Talgarreg
Ceredigion
SA44 4HB

Broken Sleep Books Ltd
Fair View
St Georges Road
Cornwall
PL26 7YH

Contents

go, go, go, said the bird: human kind
cannot bear very much reality

FLUBBERGUST

can't come out today—
bit of a mad one

i was opening a packet of crisps
and found a blue whale inside

i said: normally the packaging
is inside *you*

but he failed to see the funny side

i called a number
on the crisp packet
but i don't think the girl was listening

she said it should go out with the general waste

i said for the love of god

it's still alive

RIDERS ON THE STORM

we took our sea legs—we needed
them—up here, on the crow's nest.
look out. we'll make it better.
up here on the rafters. we'll make it
home. biblical, apocalyptic,
we waited to be saved—
somehow we survived. our house,
it's ours now, uprooted itself, tore free
from the ground, rode the tidal.
we felt sick—felt sick at first.
now, we're used to it—as i said,
we took to the sea life, harpooning
sealife, drinking sweat, eating moonlight.
i have learned to read the stars.
when you are older i will
tell you what they told me.

HOOK, LINE & SINKER

i sold a kidney, put everything
on black. i don't fit. a war
we started.

with all my sins at 4am.
i never had a fall
at work.

hate to interrupt you, but.
i think you got
the wrong idea.

you, who left
too many holes,
how the hell

you get my number?
not for pride, the wife,
one last chance,

i was sure
i'd buried you.
every day called

how to pay. you know
how to make me
want you.

NO HAVEN

the storm was a once in a hundred years kind of an affair.
it tore rocks off the cliff face, peeled skin from beach;
exposing a jungle of dead wood, shipwrecks,
buried treasure, fossilised remains and ghosts.

about the same time, we lost
our heads, down at the shore
one night. the stars looked
closer in a far flung sky. no city:

wind free to do its thing:
a dangerous kind of unleashed.
we had tethered ourselves
not far from shore,

where we got a good look
as parts of cliff
crashed
against waves.

i'd be lying if i said
when i held you
i felt more
than rattling bones.

THE KIDS

the kids are sleeping when you leave them
with an imprint on their foreheads,
and bruise their tiny hearts.
> *will they be healed on your return?*

no one can see the weight you carry.
you walk through airport security,
shown naked as they scan you.
> does it show you are a father?
> that you left your kids at home?

you talk into your smartphone.
you smile into the camera.
the kids are getting older.
technology is good.

hush little baby, daddy's here.
> i'm walking on a sandy beach.
> another day off, another day
> the world has called-in-sick.

> i'm out of signal,
> don't know where i am.
> there's so much sand, so much time.
>> *if you're doing it for something, do it for them.*

>> not all sacrifices can be seen.
>> — yours, or theirs, or mine.

A HOT MESS ON A PAVEMENT OF COLD STONE

i befriended
and pushed away
some of the best
of the worst of people.

tore thru my best
skin like paper.
under bare skies
i danced on dirt.

stars, every one
that ever lived,
fell like birds.

i put them in the pockets
of my blue jeans.

but, of course
you don't believe me.
you weren't there.

those stars meant more
than space and time and shit to me.

as long as it stays mine i guess
it's something
i can wrap around my neck
and swing from.

NOTHING LIKE THE BROCHURE

looking for something
uncomplicated, the agent said
it was *untouched, a virgin
forest.* we had to go a long way
to find a corner
of the island where
mystery met adventure.
a coral garden under
a waterfall. we bought
our ticket, stood in line,
to tap the source, to kiss
the mouth. her lips
were cracked, her teeth
were stained, her tongue
was black from sugar.
when she laughed
we were told to move
over to the foyer.
thirsty, we bought
a soda. waited
for the tide to take
us home.

THE GAME

my daughter holds
a red building block to her cheek,

says: *hello*. i pick up
another brick, say: *hello*.

no daddy, she says, taking my hand,
you're in London.

she walks me to the bedroom;
goes out; closes the door.

i put my ear
to the receiver of the block.

i can hear her through the door.
hello. brick heavy in my hand.

i miss you. my hand against my head.
when are you coming home?

i tell her soon. i tell her
i'm on the airplane. i break down

the bedroom door. holding
my arms out like an airplane;

fly around the front room;
land in the front garden;

run to the front door.
my daughter runs to me

kicking toys across the floor.
i hold her in my arms.

it's a silly game
but it feels good

to make a game of it
at last.

SCAVENGER

just before i hit the ground, my arms
opened up in fiery feathers

& i soared above the horrid roofs
of this dead end town.

i spun in circles, loop-the-loops,
dived down to the street;

squawked at people, people shooed me,
flailing their arms, i just laughed.

between bites of flesh, i cawed out:
how'd you like me now?

i took my wings towards the sun,
circled the horizon.

the northern lights evaporated, seed
turned to hay beneath my shadow.

reckoning my prey's next move.
a storm above, a silhouette.

cast across the land below.
drawn down against the wind.

INTERLUDE

truck horn. bright headlights.
it should have hurt more than it did.
but it felt nothing like that.
it was more like diving into water.
deep & dark. not cold exactly.
a white beam of light searching
beneath the surface.

many chains & not much else.
next thing i was walking.
somebody else was talking, saying:
"is this your first time?" & laughing.
walking me towards a small boat.
an oarsman sent me across
a lake towards a doorway.

"what is this?" "nobody knows."
i walked thru, into the light.
into a hospital room.
i was covered in blood,
kicking & screaming.
whose blood is this?
whose blood is this?

UNDERNEATH THE WATERFALL

the tree is ancient / a young monk met a tiger here / a widow lit a candle / we fell off our bikes, scraped our legs / not all prayers are answered / walking thru jungle until we make it / slide into water, swim to the fall / this would be a perfect place / for a photo, a memory / or to be for a moment / your body looks perfect covered in droplets / i'm sure there's a fable, a sleeping goddess / one day all of us will meet again / by then i'll have stopped saying sorry / i add it to my food / you can hear it when i speak / but sometimes no one visits this lake / & a flower blooms & dies for nothing / sometimes a prayer is just a thought / but when i think of you / & how we checked the bikes for damage / i think it could have been a perfect day

DIVINITY

yeah it's cheap, i know
this shroud i took
from the sun, ungood
my god, i bottle tears
of blood, naysayers
proclaim it rust
leaking from pipework.
but who do *you* trust?

i swear 'e came to me, told me
to do this. i take it serious.
mockery the sincerest form
of humility. the joke's on me,
a minor sin. not to sound
pushy but it's good for ya,
immaculate cure for all
modern ailments.

the world is failing
but some must be saved:
bees, birds & big cats,
wildflowers & coral reefs.
there's room for ya if y'd only
open yr mind to the power of the sun
& surrender. don't be dumb.
you feel it. become a believer.

DEPARTURE

a man & a woman
drinking coffee.

sitting close together
as if sharing a secret.

next to him, an oversized suitcase
with a haphazard handle and four wonky wheels.

next to her,
a daybag.

his is a face exhausted of options.
hers is the face you dream & wake up to.

they drink slowly
as if they could stop time by savouring flavour,

talk in short, sudden bursts
then settle into silence.

they have so much to say
& so much they can't.

he wants to promise—she hushes
his lips with her index finger.

their time is up.
they stand together.

he clutches her like something he can't quit,
her head on his chest.

he inhales deeply.
she smells of home.

A SPINNING TOP, MAYBE

a
-kindly-
kind-of-ener
gy-can-lift-a-car-a
-finger-run-into-a-burn
ing-building-blocks-hung
over-no-doubt-winning-fa
ther-of-the-crawl-across-a-
mad-expanse-of-carpet-til
ing-vomit-garden-insects
-trapped-beneath-toy-
car-in-flames-a-su
per-human-sup
er-strength-
drunk-on
-paren
tal-
lo
v
e

THE APPRENTICESHIP

i arrived there at ten to eight in the morning,
an industrial estate just off junction 4.
i parked my bike, straightened my shirt,
and knocked – three times as instructed.

a man opened the door, introduced himself as Matthew.
he'd spent his whole life manufacturing doors,
said it was the best job in the world
as no two doors are the same,

in that no two doors will open into or out of
the same space, to the same people, at the same time.

over the next three months Matthew taught me
everything he knew (about doors, at least).
until one day, he didn't show up.
the next day he didn't show up either.

i went to his house. knocked
and called his name and waited.
no answer so i let myself in.

inside, all the doors—on cupboards,
on cabinets, on wardrobes—were open;
Matthew had been looking for something.

they found his car a few days later
—all the doors were open—but they never found him.

CUTE TORNADO

/

my daughter carries around
a pet cloud
on a piece of string

she pretends it's a dinosaur
called Bronco

one time
she let go of the string
i had to chase that cloud
all around the neighbourhood

i was jumping
from roof to roof
to catch that cloud

almost lost my
footing a few times,
building blocks
tumbling down
to the floor

//

my daughter's purple boots
are magic: she walks up
walls, across the ceiling—
sits in a green umbrella

she's pulled the showerhead
downstairs from the bathroom
placed it on the floor
in the sitting room

(it's my own fault
for buying a 40-meter-long
shower cord)

and she turns the tap on
and it rains up to the ceiling
and she sits in her umbrella
and the water starts to fill up
down from the ceiling

and she bobs up and down
in her green umbrella
with a waterproof smile

fishing rubber
ducks until
teatime

///

one night i
came home from work

was knocked back by a surge of noise
swept up in the umbrella

my daughter's laugh: *daddy, let's go!*

we were swept along
the garden path
down river
to the ocean

drifted under tealight skies
to the edge of the Earth

my daughter whistled
and we were saved
by a dinosaur called Bronco

just as we were almost lost
like car keys
down the sofa

making my way through the mall. too many people. someone had left a volcano smoldering away — some sort of an exhibit on tectonics. of course, Sod's Law, the volcano erupted. the floor was lava, so i went up to the sports store, bought myself a boat-without-paddle. i rode the escalator on a sea of lava. it made me hungry, all that lava, so i went to McDonalds but the queue was too long & the rabble made me nauseous. by then a pit was festering in my stomach so i went to a street food vendor outside the mall, squeezed hot sauce all over my fingers & clapped my hands together. the ground started shaking so i called for a taxi, put my boat on the roof, said: take me to town. i told the driver i'd waited til spring for the flowers to bloom. he looked at me like i was nothing. he took me to town. there were so many people. a circus or a parade or a shootout was happening. i don't own a gun so i held out my hands, leaned my head back & fired fake shots into the high street. i imagined the police circling me, shouting through loudspeakers. when the bars closed, everyone went home & i lay on my back on the concrete, watching ash gently carpet everything in sight.

BATMAN & ROBIN

walking thru town today i see a guy dressed as Batman, climbing a high-rise.

stood in the street is a guy dressed as Robin.

do you know that guy? i say, motioning up to Batman.

Robin just looks at me & smiles.

i try to interpret the smile, but it could mean—yeah i know him—no, i don't—what do you think?

what's he doing? i ask, & Robin smiles—Fathers For Justice—fighting crime—hell if i know.

is he OK?—he's a professional—i think he's depressed—he just wants to see his kid.

a crowd forms. some jeer, some cheer. Robin just stands & smiles.

Batman turns, waves—hi guys—fuck you, Susan—help me.

& then he—falls—flies—unfurls a banner.

& Robin smiles & smiles & smiles

as Batman hits the street.

BUKOWSKI IN THE RAIN

i read a collection
of Bukowski poems
outside in
the rain
last night.

it started off
spitting but
soon became
a downpour.

in his poem about
an orchestra:
playing
in a deluge:
everyone abandons
the concert
to escape
the storm.

except for one man,
who stays because
he wants to hear
the music.

as i read
the pages became wet and torn.
the ink ran off the page,

over the grass
and down the gutter
until there were no pages,
no words,
just the outside cover,
Bukowski smiling,
and me, drenched
to the bone.

having slept off a fever,
i woke up to a sunny day
and it seemed the words of Bukowski
had gotten into the
water system:

every man was fighting,
cursing,
drinking,
every woman
showing a little more
leg than usual,

not a soul
in the neighbourhood
got out of bed
before noon,

and the
bluebird
in my
heart wasn't
weeping.

GOAT EYE WISDOM

i knew what you were thinking
you scuffed up dust at 6am

a harsh weight on my skull
a bell around your heathen neck

you said the world is ending
i said how would we even know

you said when things stop moving
i hope you stay close

115MPH

when my best friend told me
how close he came
to taking a step
into the great unknown

after losing a hell
of a lot of dough
on online roulette
in one long night

i swear i felt
a rush of air
same as he felt
the train rushed by

if i could say
anything my
words would
drown in the

sound of
the train
rushing
by

LOVE IN THE AGE OF EXTINCTION

hot day on her lips,
record breaking thighs.
no ice left when she tells me
—we need a circular economy.

she breaks the bones in my fingers,
feeds me water—filtered—thru a paper
straw. straddles me, hushes my concerns
about this aging population.

she knows love's impossible, keeps
sandbags stacked against the door.
we can't die out like dinosaurs—she
says—we are god's chosen creatures.

but her laugh, a tipping point.
she drills me until she strikes oil.
we spill across the bedroom floor.
smoke like chimneys after.

she says: the future's out on Mars.
—i don't think we'll make it.
when she's gone my cat brings me
birds fallen from the sky.

BAREFOOT & BLACKED OUT

my love graceful
falling thru
the sunset of
my living room

her heartbeat
her bodyswing
i hold her say
remember me

her sweat is blurred
against my skin
she smiles a walk
of memories

i'm laughing cos
she's laughing as
the walls fade to
an ambersand

WILDFIRE

i don't burn
books. i only
sear the edges.

in my view words
should sprawl over
the page. white space

should be extinguished.
a feral flame devouring
silence — leaving only

words. i put my pen in
the river, let ink spill.
if i didn't? i would

drown in thought.
no safety net, no
backpedal. i say:

so far so good.
up until i hit
it head on.

EVERYBODY'S ALWAYS TRYING TO SELL YOU SOMETHING

when women approach me in the street
to offer me an eye test, or to ask me
to adopt a llama, or to step inside
a converted public toilet that now offers
bite sized sausage rolls or the promise of
eternal life, i always tell them, i am late.

one of these women held my hand in hers,
looked me in the eye & said: "be precious
with your time. everyone invests in time but time
is a finite resource." i had no idea what she meant.
i shook her off my leg, ran home, locked my door,
hid behind the sofa in the dark for several years.

                    when i emerged
it was morning. i had clumps of her hair in my hands,
even bits of her scalp. i thought she was clingy,
but i remember now — it was me
who would not let go of her.

THE SPACE BETWEEN OUR HEARTS

i like to think of space and time
as a ball of yarn, which means
the space between
you and me
is not infinite. it means
i could almost touch you—
all i need to do, is fold
the corners of the room,
wrap myself into the years.
what is space anyway? who's to say
we're not still together? if
we could see things differently
maybe we could see there is
no space between us.

THE LOST TRACK

paper is murky. just when you think
it has settled, something will come along,
kick up dust. it's like staring at the sun
while holding your head underwater.
it's walking over your ceiling. believing
this is the moment, finally the moment
where nothing will ever change.

scissors catch the moonlight. holding water
in your hands. we the undertow, caught in the flow.
shadows against a light we stare into. we are counter
to the laws of things. all we know is we will die.
but we don't know what it means. memory fades
as we move away from what we have
spent our lives contemplating.

stone is ours to trade for things we want.
a precious commodity. we will never get back
the game we lost. we can almost feel it falling by.
almost taste it, almost touch it. how sweet
to know we almost knew. only an echo
if we sit still and recall what it looks like,
how it feels. it was almost ours.

SPEECH THERAPY

our language came down in the last rain,
meaning our meaning crawls and pulls
at the coattails of experience.

always at its best when asking
what is this?

*

our language came last of our senses.
an afterthought when our taste buds failed
to tell of danger, to separate
a legend from the shock of thunder.

*

our language is flint and steel
struck in a cave.
not light
but giver of light.

our caves are full of books.
the TV, the stereo's on.
we have so many ways
to say we're not alone.

*

our language is a river that goes nowhere,
a tangled knot,
a lump of ice in your whiskey throat.

our language is as sweet
and melts as quickly
as nostalgia and memory.

our language was invented
to describe things
that were born before us
and will outlive us all.

*

we must learn ancient curses
to honor the past

and pick up the cuss words
of the youth.

so that we, with bile flaming
in our stomachs,

can pass
our story
forwards.

ANY DAY NOW

when the sun rises you best be ready.
a passport, a gun, five thousand dollars.
keep telling yourself you can start anew.
life begins in your head. count to ten.

a passport, a gun, four thousand dollars.
you must follow the system. please sign here.
keep telling yourself nothing is real.
it will never happen to you.

you're not on the system. please wait here.
a finger presses a panic button.
what happens next is anybody's guess.
the sound of rain. the aftermath.

a finger squeezes, a trigger, deletes.
air escapes your lungs, birds fly.
the sound of rain. and after that?
the sun rises, a new day starts.

ACKNOWLEDGEMENTS

a number of these poems have previously been published
by Eat the Storms, Green Ink, London Grip, Impractical
Things, Telegraph Online, Gloucestershire Poetry Society,
Anthropocene, Cape, Magma, Poetry Salzburg, Amsterdam
Quarterly, Adriatic Mag, Ink Drinkers, Sieren, Black Flowers,
Frogmore Papers, Alchemy Spoon, Pidgeonholes, Acid Bath,
Acropolis.

thank you to Colin Waterman, Jack Warren, and Ina Cariño for
reading early drafts of some of these poems.

thank you Aaron Kent, Stuart McPherson, and all at Broken Sleep
Books.

special thanks to Shawn Berman, Louise Mather, Marvin
Thompson, John Morrish, Anna Saunders, Clive Oseman, Nick
Lovell, Peter & Josephine Lay, my wife and daughters, my family
and friends.

LAY OUT YOUR UNREST

Milton Keynes UK
Ingram Content Group UK Ltd.
UKHW041035110224
437582UK00005B/270